Original title:
Orange Glow

Copyright © 2025 Creative Arts Management OÜ
All rights reserved.

Author: Micah Sterling
ISBN HARDBACK: 978-1-80586-308-3
ISBN PAPERBACK: 978-1-80586-780-7

Apricot Skies

Balloons float high, like silly pies,
Chasing the clouds with goofy sighs.
Laughter bursts like fireflies bright,
Wiggling through the soft twilight.

Jelly beans rain from the sun,
Kids run around, oh what fun!
Twirling in circles, dizzy and loud,
Wearing our best, we're feeling proud.

Luminous Echoes

Bouncing beams sneak through the trees,
Whispering giggles carried by breeze.
Silly shadows dance on the ground,
Making us jump, spinning around.

Every chuckle a sparkling shout,
As ducks in a pond wiggle about.
The fish wear hats, oh what a sight,
In this carnival of pure delight.

Saffron's Embrace

In the kitchen, pancakes flip,
Syrup rivers, let it drip!
Butterflies join the breakfast show,
Sipping tea from cups aglow.

Jam jars giggle as they stack,
One tumbles over, what a crack!
Spilling fun with every bite,
Morning magic, pure delight.

Golden Hour Serenade

Kites sail high in the laughing breeze,
Whirling and twirling with such ease.
Silly hats dance on heads so bright,
Chasing the shadows, oh what a sight!

As the sun dips low, colors collide,
Crayons laughing, nowhere to hide.
Bringing joy, a vivid parade,
Every moment a playful charade.

Dusk's Painterly Touch

The sky with splashes bright and bold,
Like a fruit salad, vibrant and gold.
Clouds dance and swirl, a silly sight,
As day gives way to a burst of light.

Laughter echoes as shadows leap,
A playful game that won't let us sleep.
The sun winks down with a cheeky grin,
Saying, 'Come on, let the fun begin!'

Milking the moment, the horizon laughs,
Squirting hues like colorful gaffs.
Colors drip like ice cream cones,
Oh, how we giggle at the sky's funny tones!

So we chase the sun as it slips away,
In a game of tag, we beg it to stay.
With each fading ray, a chuckle we find,
In the sky's brilliant show, we're forever entwined.

Last Light's Affection

When daylight fades, the silliness reigns,
As the backdrop bursts with fruity stains.
Sunbeams bounce like kids on a swing,
The day doesn't end; it just wants to cling.

The clouds wear hats, big and round,
While blushing rays dance all around.
Even the stars roll their eyes and say,
'What a show! Let's join the play!'

Crickets chirp their own funny tune,
In a concert featuring the fading moon.
With vibrant hues that tickle the sight,
Every color grins under the twilight.

As night tiptoes in with a giggle so sly,
We wave our goodbyes to the brightening sky.
Last light's embrace is warm and light,
A silly farewell, as day turns to night.

Tones of the Evening Sun

In the sky, a jester's grin,
With bright hues that make us spin.
The world laughs, a canvas wide,
As day dances, and dusk glides.

Citrus balls roll down the lane,
Tickling toes, oh what a game!
With giggles in the twilight's hem,
The sun plays tricks, oh yes, my friend.

Lively Shades of Twilight

In the dusk, the hues take flight,
Chasing shadows, what a sight!
Giggling clouds, they float and tease,
As crickets croon, they do as they please.

The garden glows, a silly show,
With flaming dragons, watch them go!
They twirl and dance, oh what a spree,
In the breeze, so wild and free!

Illuminated Silhouettes

Figures prance in the dim light,
With laughter echoing through the night.
The moon winks at the stars so bright,
As shadows play, what a delight!

On the stage of twilight's play,
Silly antics lead the way.
With secrets shared, and whispers low,
In the glow, how funny they grow!

Citrus Sunsets

When the sky becomes a peachy dome,
Even squirrels dance, feeling at home.
Bubbles float on the saffron breeze,
With giggles spilling through the trees.

The day's a fruit, juicy and bright,
With silly shapes in fading light.
As laughter ripples in the air,
Even flowers can't help but share!

Glimmers of Twilight

The sky drips with nectar,
A painter's crazy brush,
Ducks wearing sunglasses,
As ducks tend to rush.

Squirrels breeze past the swings,
With acorn hats on their heads,
They dance in silly circles,
On the swings, they take beds.

Fireflies join the parade,
With little glowing feet,
They sip on light lemonade,
As night begins to greet.

Laughter spills in the air,
Jokes tossed like a frisbee,
Under the glow that's near,
Just watch, it's quite windy!

Flames in the Evening

A grill's roaring like a lion,
Hot dogs doing the dance,
While burgers flip without trying,
In a barbecue romance.

Kids run wild with painted faces,
Chasing shadows like dreams,
While adults play musical chairs,
In silly, playful teams.

The sun winks before it fades,
As cats sing the night tune,
And socks slide down the raides,
In a starry cartoon.

Laughter lights up the park,
Like sparklers in the gloom,
As friends share tales 'til dark,
With adventures that bloom!

Fires of Autumn

Leaves tumble in the air,
As trees sneeze bright colors,
The pumpkins join the fair,
Among the giggling hollers.

Squirrels wear tiny hats,
As they scurry and play,
Juggling acorns like cats,
In a comical way.

The wind sings silly tunes,
As scarves float like balloons,
And everyone shares snacks,
With silly, crazy laughs.

Jumping in piles of cheer,
A symphony of fun,
As the crisp air draws near,
'Til the last joke's begun!

The Warmth Lingers

Cozy blankets piled high,
As the sun begins to yawn,
A cat draped like a spy,
On the couch, soft as dawn.

Friends trade muffled laughter,
Wrapped snug in knitted threads,
With stories that come after,
As warmth spills from their heads.

Teacups dance on the table,
With biscuits on the side,
All giggles, can't be stable,
As silliness takes pride.

The day ends in a glow,
With memories in a mix,
Underneath the sly show,
Of antics and cool tricks!

Amber Embrace

In evening's light, where silly smiles grow,
A cat in a hat puts on quite the show.
Jumping in circles, it dances with flair,
While a dog with a tie looks up, unaware.

Teabags in hand, we sip lemonade fast,
Playing charades, the chuckles will last.
The sun spills its juice on our picnic spread,
As crumbs fly like confetti above our heads.

Luminous Dusk

The fireflies twirl, like tiny disco balls,
While squirrels wear shades, ignoring the calls.
With marshmallows roasting amidst joyful shouts,
A raccoon steals snacks, creating big doubts.

A dance-off erupts by the juice jug's side,
As everyone giggles and takes in the ride.
When shadows grow long, we laugh and we tease,
And the breeze plays the music, as light leaves its tease.

Coral Reflections

In puddles of laughter, our thoughts take a splash,
As seagulls perform their impeccable dash.
A crab with a swagger, it struts to its beat,
While flip-flops are flying on unsuspecting feet.

The sunset is painted with ketchup and fries,
As we feast on cool stories and share silly lies.
A starfish named Fred does the limbo with glee,
While beach bums unite for a dance by the sea.

Tangerine Hues

With zesty adventures, our laughter takes flight,
As sneaky fruit drinks sneak into the night.
A monkey on bikes takes a whirl with great zeal,
While ducks crack wise with their quacks that reveal.

Under a swirl of citrus confetti,
The fun never slows, and nobody's petty.
We toast to the sunset, our cups filled with cheer,
As life throws its colors, we echo, 'Oh dear!'

Golden Whispers

The sun wore a crown of marmalade,
With buttered toast on parade.
Birds in the sky did a silly dance,
While squirrels planned their nutty romance.

Lemonade laughter bounced off the trees,
Tickling the leaves with a gentle tease.
A cat dressed in shades, laid back on the lawn,
Spinning lazy tales until dusk's yawn.

Flames of Serenity

A campfire flickered like a cheeky grin,
As marshmallows roasted, oh where to begin?
The fireflies buzzed with their glow-in-the-dark,
While ants held a meeting—an anarchist spark.

Jokes floated high on the summer's breeze,
With laughter erupting, a tickle of tease.
S'mores induced giggles, and chocolatey smears,
As we shared our secrets over campfire cheers.

Sunkissed Horizons

On the coast where the giggles blend,
The waves tease the sand in a playful trend.
With surfboards ready and sunscreen smeared,
We dashed to the water, no one interfered.

Seagulls swooped down for a fry or two,
As sun hats flew off, into skies so blue.
With beach ball battles and the splashes loud,
We danced like kids, oh, we were so proud.

Dusk's Warm Embrace

As day turned to night, we spun like tops,
With shadows sneaking in, and friendly hops.
The twilight giggled, pulling us close,
While crickets began their evening dose.

Stars peeked out with a wink in their eyes,
Making funny faces, oh what a surprise!
We strolled hand in hand with a candy flare,
While night wrapped us up in its cozy snare.

A Tapestry of Warmth

In the kitchen, the chef's on a spree,
Pasta in orange, a sight to see.
Carrots are dancing, potatoes in line,
Eating this dinner feels like I'm divine.

Cats wear sombreros, strutting with flair,
Chasing a rogue chipmunk, what a wild stare!
The dog joins the party, tail wagging so fast,
In this quirky kitchen, good luck will last!

Fragrant Skies

Juicy citrus off the tree,
Squeeze it on pancakes, lemon spree!
The neighbors all giggle, their faces so bright,
As juice splatters funny, laughter takes flight.

Kites in the air, all burst into cheer,
One got tangled with a pineapple sphere!
As we feast on a picnic, ants join the fun,
Stealing our snacks as we bask in the sun.

Beneath the Radiant Veil

Wearing bright hats, we stroll down the street,
With colors so vibrant, it's hard to compete.
A dog in a tutu steals all the stares,
While kids toss confetti, they don't have a care.

A clown juggles jellybeans, oh what a sight!
Accidentally hits a bird mid-flight.
With laughs all around, like a sitcom scene,
Life's silly moments are fit for a queen.

Melodies of the Setting Sun

Crickets are singing, but off-key today,
As frogs join in chorus, they're stuck in a play.
Under skies fading, that whimsical hue,
We witness a band that's led by a zoo!

A raccoon on drums, while a bear plays guitar,
They serenade us from near and far.
With smiles and giggles filling the air,
This twilight concert is beyond compare!

Copper Reverie

In a kitchen bright and lively,
A pot jumped, oh so sprightly.
Carrots danced upon the stove,
In a vibrant, veggie grove.

The garlic clapped, the onions cheered,
As cheeky spices boldly steered.
A sprinkle here, a dash of fun,
Dinner's not done until we run!

The table set with laughter's grace,
Each dish adorned a quirky face.
Friends all giddy, bright and bold,
Sharing tales of mischief told.

As we feast beneath the light,
In this kitchen, joy ignites!
With every bite, a giggle bursts,
Transforming meals into wild firsts.

Dawn's Gentle Blaze

As morning breaks with laughter's hymn,
The coffee pot wears a grin.
Toast pops up like a jack in box,
With butter spreading joy like flocks.

Eggs a-sunny with a tease,
They wobble on the plate with ease.
Bacon strips like dancers twirl,
In this cheerful breakfast swirl.

The juice is laughing, orange cheeked,
Sipping slow, the giggles peaked.
We toast to mornings bright and fun,
Before we dash, the day's begun.

With smiles wide, we claim the day,
In this kitchen, where we play.
From dawn to dusk, the joy won't dip,
Our lives a vibrant, hearty trip!

Cantaloupe Canvas

In the garden where fruits collide,
A cantaloupe begins to glide.
With giggles green and laughter sweet,
It's a party that can't be beat!

Peaches prance like royalty,
Sweeping through with jubilee.
Tomatoes roll in laughter's glow,
Creating chaos, don't you know?

With melons singing silly songs,
Together where the fruit joy throngs.
Bananas slip on laughter's slip,
As the whole garden begins to flip!

From vine to vine, a fruity chase,
In every corner, smiles embrace.
Each bite a burst of giggling zest,
In this canvas, joy's the guest.

Incandescent Embrace

A bulb overhead starts to jig,
With every flick, it plays a gig.
Shadows dance across the wall,
In this bright space, we have a ball.

The lamp in the corner cracks a joke,
While the sofa shakes and lovingly pokes.
With every flicker, giggles bloom,
Chasing worries out of the room.

Curtains sway like limbs in glee,
Draping colors for all to see.
The rug spins tales beneath our feet,
Enticing us to skip and greet.

So here's to laughter and the light,
In this embrace, all feels right.
With every twinkle, fun takes flight,
In incandescent joy, we unite!

Threads of Daylight

A cat dances in the sun,
While birds chirp, just for fun.
Socks mismatched on a sleepy friend,
Morning mischief has no end.

Pancakes flip with a happy flop,
Sticky syrup, we can't stop.
Giggles burst like morning rays,
Life's a laugh in so many ways.

Lingering Dusk

The sky wears a funny hat,
It twirls and swirls like a cartoon cat.
Chasing shadows, the kids all squeal,
As fireflies dance, making it surreal.

A sneaky raccoon steals some pie,
While grandma's laughing, oh my, oh my!
Crickets serenade the cheery crowd,
Dusk takes a bow, feeling proud.

Warm Ember Thoughts

S'mores melting by the fire,
We plot our mischief, never tire.
Chocolate's gooey, laughter's sweet,
Our evening's mix feels like a treat.

Ghost stories flip to silly tales,
With giggles echoing through the gales.
A marshmallow fight, oh what a sight,
As shadows dance in the fading light.

Lasting Luminescence

With glow sticks waving, we start to play,
Funky disco moves, we sway and sway.
A sock on a hand, a hat on a foot,
Inside the glow, we're all a hoot!

The night is young, our spirits high,
As laughter sparkles against the sky.
We'll dance 'til dawn, with dreams aglow,
In our little world, we steal the show.

Nectar Tints of Dusk

The sun dips low, a fruit on fire,
Chasing shadows, quenching desire.
Sipping light from cups so round,
Bumbling bees buzzing all around.

Lemonade jokes in the twilight shine,
A backpack full of giggles, oh so fine!
Bad puns flutter, like moths to light,
As stars come out, the laughs take flight.

Coral Dreams

In a coral sky, where laughter flows,
Fish in tuxedos, do the tango shows.
With jellybean trees and candy streams,
We dance with the squids in our wildest dreams.

Prancing around with custard pies,
Slip on a banana, oh what a surprise!
Ticklish tickles from the breezy air,
As we giggle at seagulls without a care.

Glowed by Fire

The campfire crackles with stories old,
S'mores go flying, a sight to behold.
Ghosts made of marshmallows, dancing around,
Tales of the silly, breaking the ground.

Droopy hot dogs, on sticks they prance,
While fireworks giggle and start their dance.
We roast our fears and toast to the night,
With a spark of joy, everything feels right.

Sunkissed Canvas

A canvas stretched where giggles bloom,
Splashing hues in a sunny room.
With paintbrushes bouncing, colors collide,
Creating a masterpiece, silly with pride.

Palettes of laughter, splatters of glee,
Dancing in shades of happy esprit.
As puddles of joy overflow the frame,
Every brushstroke is a chuckle, a game!

Saffron Serenade

In a pot of curry dreams, they sing,
Spicy jokes with a twist in spring.
Laughter simmers, bubbles bright,
Tickled taste buds take flight.

Pineapple hats and mango shoes,
Dance on tables with silly views.
Giggling grains of rice align,
In a feast that's quite divine.

Carrots chuckle, peas do prance,
Radishes join, the veggies dance.
Chopping boards with playful glee,
Sing a tune of jubilee.

As the saffron swirls and flows,
Creating moments that everyone knows.
Laughter's recipe starts to show,
In this funny, colorful glow.

Illuminated Silence

Under neon lights, we collide,
Whispers echo where secrets hide.
Bright bulbs spark when heads are turned,
In the glow, our laughter burned.

Shadows play their silly games,
Darkness tries to hide their names.
In the stillness, a giggle flares,
Lighting up our funny affairs.

The glow from the fridge, what a sight,
Daring snacks in the dead of night.
Mischief brewing on midnight's stage,
As dreams turn into a funny page.

With each buzz of the silly light,
We revel in the soft delight.
Chasing silence in bright disguise,
We dance under the knowing skies.

Rusted Skylight

The old roof creaks with tales to tell,
Where laughter lingers, all is well.
A skylight cracks with shades of fun,
Letting in rays, on us they run.

Pigeons parade with pompous flair,
Beneath the rust, they float in air.
Jokes shatter like dust from the beams,
Creating chaos, igniting dreams.

Rays poke through like fingers bright,
Tugging hearts with sheer delight.
As colors spill across the floor,
We giggle at the creaky lore.

In this old house where echoes stay,
We make the silly moments play.
With rusted tales and laughter's draw,
Life shines bright in every flaw.

Solar Sigh

The bright balloon slips from my hand,
Floats away like a whimsical band.
Chasing it down, I trip and slide,
Into a puddle, oh what a ride!

Sunshine giggles through green leaves,
As a bug dances in morning eves.
It winks at me from a petal's side,
With a twirl and a flutter, it won't hide.

Umbrella drinks and lemon pies,
Together we concoct the silliest lies.
Each sip a spark, each bite a cheer,
In this sunny world, we have no fear.

And as we bask in the glowing heat,
Life's little hiccups make it sweet.
With every smile and cheeky sigh,
We paint the day beneath the sky.

Blazing Twilight

At sunset, the sky's a disaster,
Like a fruit salad gone faster.
The clouds are in a ruckus,
Dancing like a circus!

When the day starts to wink,
Colors blend, then they stink.
A flamingo on a trampoline,
What a sight, oh so keen!

Laughter spills from evening light,
As fireflies take their flight.
They flicker like a party hat,
Brightening up the chitchat!

In this mess of laughter's gleam,
Life feels like a wild dream.
When colors clash in a spree,
You can't help but just be free!

Golden Flicker

A little lamp with a silly grin,
Flickering like it's found a twin.
Its light hops, with style and grace,
Making shadows jiggle in place.

All the ants have come around,
Hoping for a dance to be found.
They groove with beats from a snail's shell,
In a disco where they twirl so well!

A rusty bike in the golden hue,
Seems to laugh as it jigs, too.
Rust and cheer in every nook,
It's a party, just take a look!

A day that shines like butter on toast,
With joy that fills up space, we boast.
Each flicker, a burst of delight,
Turning mundane into sheer light!

Warmth of Dawn

The skies are lending us their cheer,
With a breakfast cooked by a deer.
Waffles flipping in the breeze,
Sunlight's giggles, oh, what a tease!

Roosters croon with a comic twist,
Announcing dawn with a flourish, oh bliss!
They tiptoe on their clucking toes,
While the sleepy cat just dozes and dozes.

Caffeine spills from a teacup tree,
While happy squirrels chant with glee.
Every leaf does a little jig,
Nature dancing, oh so big!

As day breaks, riding a playful kite,
Out comes the fun, shining so bright.
In this warmth, a joyful mime,
Savoring moments, oh so sublime!

Vermilion Echoes

A parrot sings in a fancy hat,
Saying 'hello' to a quirky cat.
With vermilion feathers, such flair,
They start a jam without a care.

The trees shake with playful vibes,
Crackling laughs and silly jibes.
Even the rocks join in the fun,
Rolling around under the sun!

A runaway balloon takes a bow,
Hopping by, waving, 'What's up now?'
Squirrels' acrobats, in the air,
Chasing giggles, without a care!

As echoes bounce in a comedic show,
The world brightens with each blow.
In these moments, oh so sweet,
Life's a dance, can't miss a beat!

Fiery Horizons

The sky's a spicy fruit salad,
Giggling clouds prance like mad,
Tangerine laughs as lemons grin,
Even the sun wears a goofy skin.

Bouncing rays hit the big ole tree,
It's doing a dance, oh so carefree,
Branches wave like they just won the sweep,
While shadows below take a cheeky leap.

With every glow, the critters cheer,
Squirrels juggle acorns, full of good cheer,
Laughter echoes through this bright show,
Who knew dusk had such a funny glow?

A flamingo in shades, what a sight!
Trying to disco in the fading light,
Dancing with friends, they're quite the crew,
Under the giggles of the brightening hue.

Citrus Dreams at Dusk

In the twilight, fruits start their chat,
Lemons in hats, oh where's the cat?
Lime jokes trade as the sun waves goodbye,
Pineapples laugh, reaching for the sky.

A citrus parade, with zest on a roll,
Mandarins whirling, they're on a stroll,
Twisting and turning in vibrant embrace,
Time to dip into fun, a fruity race!

As the light dims, mirth expands,
Juicy giggles fill the lands,
Grapefruits juggling as they skip,
In this slice of humor, we take a trip.

With each dainty glow above our heads,
Citrus puns dance, forgetting the dreads,
Under the charm of this wacky view,
Let's toast to the laughs, dreams painted anew.

Autumn's Blush

Leaves in hues of a citrus feast,
Swaying gently, inviting the beast,
Pumpkins chuckle, rolling away,
While the harvest moon starts its play.

A scarecrow grins with a corn-cob hat,
Trying to shoo away a fat little brat,
Squirrels squeal at the autumn's tease,
Nibbling treats like it's a breeze.

In this orchard of giggles and cheer,
Every fruit has a story to share,
Grapes sneaking sips, daring the glare,
While apples burst forth, tossing their hair.

As dusk blankets this funny old show,
With rustling leaves and a gentle glow,
We gather 'round, laughter no rush,
In the fall's embrace, nature's soft blush.

Warmth of Harvest

Under the sun, all creatures prance,
Beets and carrots take up the dance,
Radishes twirl, quite proud in their patch,
While the corn stalks giggle, good friends to catch.

Merriment swells in the golden field,
Each ear of corn a secret revealed,
Pumpkins parade with curls and cheer,
Bouncing around like they own the sphere.

Baskets overflowing, laughter's the plan,
Tomatoes blushing, they're part of the clan,
Harvest moon glows, keeping a watch,
On the happy farmers, when they're in a scotch.

In this laughter, the season's delight,
With every bounty, the spirits ignite,
So let's throw a party, no reason to wait,
In the warmth of harvest, love's on our plate.

Radiant Horizons

A sunbeam slipped on a banana peel,
It laughed and danced, oh what a deal!
Mangoes grinned from a nearby tree,
As they juggled oranges, wild and free.

Skies painted with a bright party hat,
Clouds were bouncing, imagine that!
Lemons joined in the silly parade,
Shining brightly, they all got laid.

Firelight Lullaby

A campfire flickered, telling a joke,
It spit some sparks, and the marshmallows spoke.
'We're sweet and gooey, don't waste our chance,
To twirl with crackers, let's have a dance!'

S'mores on the grill, doing the twist,
Chocolates melting, they can't resist.
When laughter erupts from the starry dome,
Even weenies sigh, 'This feels like home!'

Peachy Aura

In a garden filled with funny faces,
Peaches giggle in their fuzzy laces.
They wear little hats made of leaves and sun,
As squirrels plot mischief, oh what fun!

Bumblebees buzz with a witty flair,
Telling tales of pollen without a care.
A tomato blushed, caught in the mix,
Joking, 'I'm fruit too, can you fix?'

Gleaming Affection

Glowing like socks in the dryer's embrace,
Pickles are dancing all over the place!
They've found a partner, a cheeky bean,
Spinning around like they're on a scene.

A heart-shaped cookie just winked at a pie,
Said, 'Love is sweet, oh me, oh my!'
With floury hands, they shared a quick kiss,
In a kitchen full of warmth, nothing's amiss.

Radiant Reflections

A silly sunbeams dance, without a care,
They tickle the clouds, make them bare.
With laughter they flicker, like light on a joke,
Creating a canvas for all the folks.

Chase the giggles, chase the rays,
Watch those shadows play silly ways.
The skies are a canvas, wild and bright,
Painting fun with every light.

Bouncing off rooftops in a grand parade,
Even the cats join the jolly charade.
Skip along sidewalks, join in the cheer,
Under these rays, life's always dear.

Oh! What a show, in the evening's embrace,
Even grumpy old men wear a smile on their face.
So grab your popcorn and don't be slow,
Let's giggle together in this vibrant glow.

A Flourish of Flame

A goofy fireball rolls down the street,
With sparks of laughter, it can't be beat.
It whistles and whirrs like a jolly old man,
Eating too much pie, that's the plan!

Chasing the squirrels, tickling the trees,
With pranks up its sleeve, it does just as it please.
The breeze carries chuckles, away it goes,
Tickling your senses, and making you pose.

With every flare, there's a story to tell,
From giant marshmallows to a candy hotel.
Celebrating folly, giving up the shame,
Life's just a party, isn't it the same?

As day slowly ends, the fire takes flight,
Giggling with joy at the fall of the night.
So let the laughter rise like the stars up above,
With this splendid flicker, let's share the love!

Hues of Dusk

Whimsical whispers paint the sky,
Like a painter who forgot to comply.
Splashes of joy in every twist,
Like an artist's dream that can't be missed.

With winks from the sun and nods from the moon,
Every color sings a silly tune.
Shadows chase laughter, shadows chase dreams,
Here in the twilight, nothing's as it seems.

Sprightly colors tumble, skip, and sway,
Creating a spectacle, hip-hip-hooray!
Like a funny hat parade at the fair,
With jokes aplenty floating in the air.

As laughter drifts softly like leaves on a stream,
Join in the fun, share the gleam.
For under these hues, life's a grand jest,
And in this funny game, we are truly blessed.

The Luster of Evenings

At eve's embrace, the giggles rise,
Like fireflies dancing 'neath the darkening skies.
The stars wear a tutu, twinkling with flair,
While the moon shows off with a silvery stare.

Pajamas are worn, hats thrown in glee,
As night wraps around like a warm cup of tea.
With echoes of laughter bouncing off walls,
Even the streetlight joins in the calls.

Under a blanket of shimmering dreams,
Silly stories flow like bubbling streams.
And shadows break out in a tap-dance spree,
In this luster-filled evening, you and me.

So gather 'round friends, let the fun begin,
For under the stars, we'll giggle and grin.
In the glow of this night, let's laugh till we ache,
With memories shining like a night-time cake!

A Taste of Warmth

A splash of zest on my bread,
Like sunshine danced on my head.
I giggle as I spread it wide,
The flavor learns to take a ride.

Sipping juice with a silly grin,
It makes my taste buds want to spin.
Fruit salad jokes in every bite,
The breakfast table's pure delight.

A pot of stew, oh what a sight,
Its colors burst and feel just right.
My spoon does jiggles, makes me laugh,
I'm drowning in this sweet mishmash!

From laughter's zest, all joy has grown,
In every bite, my heart feels known.
With every sip and joyful bite,
This crazy meal, oh what a light!

Sunlit Canvases

Brushstrokes dance on the canvas bright,
With hues that bring such sheer delight.
The silly splashes and drips collide,
Like paint was flung from joy's wild ride.

A quirky sun with a winking eye,
Tickles clouds as they drift by.
Each daub a grin, each stroke a cheer,
Creating smiles from far and near.

The trees wear hats of yellow flair,
While flowers giggle without a care.
A landscape painted in laughter's tune,
It shines like mischief under the moon.

With every hue, a joke is told,
In vibrant tones, the warmth unfolds.
When art is fun, it's silly yet,
A canvas laughs that we won't forget!

The Last Light of Day

As daylight wanes, it starts to play,
The sky pulls pranks in a jazzy way.
A curtain drawn on the world's own stage,
Where colors giggle with every age.

Shadows stretch and start to yawn,
The sun is dressed like a silly fawn.
It tickles clouds with a golden hand,
The evening chuckles across the land.

The crickets sing a nighttime song,
As fireflies dance, it won't be long.
With every flash, a playful jest,
The night arrives in its funniest vest.

As stars pop out in a twinkling spree,
The moon plays hide and seek with glee.
In the last light, the chuckles flow,
As dreams ignite in a starry row!

Harvest Moonlight

Under the bulb that shines so bright,
Pumpkins prance in the cool moonlight.
They wear their smiles, big and round,
While critters dance upon the ground.

The scarecrow cracks his funniest joke,
And hay bales giggle, oh what a poke!
They join a party of harvest cheer,
As silly shadows start to appear.

Apples wobble on branches high,
While pears barter tales with a pie.
Laughter bubbles from every tree,
In this orchard, joy runs free!

With lanterns lit in a playful glow,
The night is young and set to go.
So join the feast of funny delight,
Under the moon's soft, gleeful light!

The Warmth of Dusk

As day bids night a cheeky grin,
The sun does dance in shades so thin.
A citrus wink from skies so bright,
With laughter spilled in fading light.

The trees wear hats of bright delight,
While squirrels tap dance, oh what a sight!
The world's a stage, a clownish play,
In every hue, the jokes ballet.

A flick of dusk's comedic flair,
The shadows stretch with no one there.
The breeze whispers puns, quite absurd,
While crickets chirp the night's last word.

As curtain drops on day's grand show,
The afterglow steals the spotlight's flow.
In twilight's giggle, we find our peace,
Tomorrow's humor will never cease.

Twilight's Citrus Embrace

When twilight swirls with zestful cheer,
A citrus hug draws everyone near.
The sky a mix of giggles and blush,
In this fruity realm, we dance and rush.

The clouds wear smiles, so fluffy and bright,
Tickling rooftops, oh what a sight!
As fireflies join with snickers and glee,
They light the way for you and me.

A tangerine tumble, a lemony lean,
The laughter fills the small in-between.
Chasing shadows with joyful shouts,
In twilight's orchard, there's no room for doubts.

With every giggle, the stars appear,
A stellar laughter, drawing us near.
In this vibrant embrace, we laugh, we sing,
Twilight's cheeriness, a wonderful fling.

Burnished Canopies

Underneath the burnished trees,
The laughter swirls on a playful breeze.
Leaves hold secrets in gold and brown,
While squirrels crack jokes, wearing their crowns.

A canopy painted with whimsy and jest,
Where shadows play and sunlight's a guest.
Each branch a stage, each fruit a laugh,
As nature joins in this silly path.

The ground is a carpet of jokes and puns,
Where giggles roll and the laughter runs.
Every breeze whispers words of delight,
In this cozy home, we dance through the night.

As dusk settles in with a wink and a shout,
The canopy laughs, there's never a doubt.
With the day's finest comedy tucked in the leaves,
We share in the fun that the evening weaves.

Flickering Horizons

Flickering hues on the horizon's edge,
A circus of colors, it's quite the pledge.
The sun juggles rays, like clowns in a row,
With skies so silly, let your laughter flow.

The horizon dances with quirky delight,
As day and night play tag in flight.
Each moment a punchline, a sweet little tease,
In the shadow play where giggles don't cease.

A playful chirp from a cheeky bird,
Sends ripples of joy, not a single word.
Bubbly clouds drift with mischievous flair,
Carrying chuckles on a bright evening air.

As the sun dips low with a curtsy and spin,
We revel in laughter, let the fun begin!
In flickering horizons, joy finds its theme,
Where silliness reigns, we all chase the dream.

Caramel Skies

The sun spills sweet from above,
Cotton candy clouds take flight,
Marshmallow dreams we all think of,
As day turns into night.

Lemonade laughs and juggled sights,
Silly friends hop here and there,
Chasing fireflies, dancing lights,
With giggles thick as summer air.

Cactus hats on fuzzy heads,
Pineapple shoes on silly feet,
We twirl, we spin, through flower beds,
In this delightful, fruity heat.

Pastel hues in sunset's cheer,
Life tastes sweeter with each glance,
We may be silly, it's quite clear,
But join us now in this great dance.

Whispers of Warmth

Toasty tales in evening glow,
Popcorn kernels start to pop,
Bouncing balls in grass below,
As buddies dive and flip and flop.

Illusions of orange, red and gold,
Playing pranks like kids at play,
Churros twist, and stories told,
Bring chuckles in the fading day.

Muffins giggle, pies take flight,
Ice cream cones on puppies' noses,
Balloons and bubbles chase the night,
As moonlight softly dozes.

Tiptoe around the crackling glow,
Where marshmallows browse and chatter,
Each laugh like sugar, sweet and slow,
In whimsical dreams, it's all that matters.

Autumn's Last Dance

Leaves like dancers in the breeze,
Wobble down in swirl and spin,
Giggling branches tease with ease,
As pumpkins wear their silly grin.

Candy corn, the taste of cheer,
In pockets deep, it finds a home,
We play hide and seek right here,
As twilight whispers, 'Let's roam!'

Scarecrows plot their silly schemes,
While pies parade in a warm jacket,
Underneath the stars, we dream,
Of turtles knitting scarlet blankets.

Costumed critters rush about,
With giggles wrapped in crisp, cool air,
In this mirthful autumn bout,
Every moment spins a fair.

Soft Stroke of Twilight

The day retreats with playful sighs,
Knitting stars with golden thread,
Whiskers twitch as night-time flies,
 Winking owls paint the sky red.

Jellybeans jump across the street,
 With traffic lights in silly hats,
A giggly creak in every treat,
As snickerdoodles wear their spats.

Pajama queens twirl in delight,
While shadows seek to play their part,
Their hands wave, sprightly, bright,
 Making mischief from the heart.

Silly dreams twinkle and swirl,
In the hues where day takes flight,
With a chuckle, the night's a pearl,
 As we shimmy into twilight.

Marmalade Skies

The sun's a big toast, so warm and bright,
Dodging clouds like a game of kite.
Birds wear shades, they think it's so cool,
While squirrels dance at the edge of the pool.

Neighbors squint, with hats pulled down,
Ice cream drips on the dog next to town.
Picnics planned with a splash of cream,
But ants join in, oh what a dream!

Kids run wild with popsicle sticks,
Chasing each other, pulling off tricks.
The sky giggles, a sunny jest,
While everyone hopes for a lazy rest.

Apricot Veil

The sun peeks shyly behind a puffy cloud,
While kids yell loudly, yelling out loud.
A cat in a hat scans the scene,
Who knew a feline could be so keen?

Lemonade rivers flow from the stand,
Cupcakes topple from a kid's hand.
Sidewalk chalk writes tales of fame,
As grandma rolls by calling each name.

The breeze is a joker, tickling the grass,
While neighbors all gather, letting time pass.
A picnic blanket becomes a grand stage,
Where squirrels perform, earning their wage.

Flame-Kissed Moments

A flamingo struts in shades of red,
Telling the turtles, 'Follow my lead!'
The sun's a grilled cheese, melting away,
Everyone's laughing, oh what a day!

Hot dogs sizzle, popcorn pops loud,
As penguins in bow ties gather around.
Ice cream cones wobble, falling down,
But smiles remain, nobody frowns.

A frisbee flies like a bird on a spree,
While kids trip over their own two feet.
The sun winks down, a mischievous tease,
In this world of fun, all feel at ease.

Honeyed Light

Honey drips from a busy bee's dance,
While ants parade in a funny trance.
The sun laughs softly, a warm golden hue,
As grandpa declares, "Let's paint it anew!"

Bad jokes are shared, old and young cheer,
As dad slips and tumbles—bring on the beer!
Lemon trees giggle, swaying with flair,
Squeaky swings squeal, it's a sight rare.

Sun hats are flopping, parents are bold,
While kids gather gold treasures, their dreams unfold.
A dog rolls over, covered in sand,
In the honeyed light, life feels so grand.

Mango Tints in the Sky

Mango stains on the horizon,
As the sun takes a dip,
Birds in flip-flops are flyin',
Time for a sunset skip.

Lemons laugh in the breeze,
While coconuts play tag,
Even the waves seem at ease,
Wearing a bright little rag.

Clouds in their fruity suits,
Dance like they know a jig,
While dolphins in fancy boots,
Twirl with a playful dig.

So grab a tropical snack,
And join the silly show,
For in this fruity crack,
Gigs flow like the mango glow.

Vibrant Sunset Serenade

The sun wears a vibrant hat,
In shades of lemon-lime,
With winks like mischievous cats,
It's playtime, oh so prime.

Sunbeams strum a beachy tune,
While waves do the conga,
The sand joins in, what a boon,
Even the crabs sing a jonga.

The horizon pulls a quick prank,
With swirls of laughter loud,
Clouds tumble, a playful flank,
In this sunset merry crowd.

As the day takes its bow,
With colors that sizzle and pop,
Let's dance like we don't know how,
For the laughter must never stop.

Dappled Glow

In the dappled light, they twirl,
Tiny critters on parade,
With wings that shimmer and swirl,
Their laughter never fades.

The daisies wear party hats,
As shadows leap in delight,
Even the squirrels do backflats,
In this playful golden light.

Branches sway like they've got groove,
Tickling the sky with glee,
While butterflies bust a move,
As joyful as can be.

So let the sun create a show,
Of whimsy and giggling trees,
In nature's dappled glow,
Life dances with the breeze.

Gingered Light

Ginger snaps through the bright air,
With a twist and a turn,
The sun makes us all aware,
That it's time to laugh and learn.

Carrots jig in the sunlight,
Rabbits join for the fun,
They hop with all of their might,
In a race 'til the day is done.

The sky glows in goofy shades,
While honey bees may just sing,
Frolicking in the glades,
Living life like a king!

So let's all join this delight,
With smiles that never part,
In the warm gingered light,
Let's dance from the heart!

Warm Strokes on the Canvas

A brush dipped in laughter,\nSwirls of zest take flight,\nPops of laughter painted bright,\nArtful chaos, what a sight!\n\nSplashes of citrus, never shy,\nDancing with joy, oh my!\nTicklish tickles on the skin,\nA masterpiece where giggles begin.\n\nSplotches here, dribbles there,\nEvery mess shows love and care,\nSketches of silliness abound,\nColorful quirks, joy unbound.\n\nIn this art, we find our muse,\nBright and silly, we can't lose,\nWith every stroke, we celebrate,\nLife's absurdity, isn't it great?

Flame-Kissed Clouds

Puffy marshmallows up above,\nKissed by giggles, warm and snug,\nChasing dreams that float like cream,\nWhat a funny, fluffy dream!\n\nBubbly clouds pop in the sky,\nWith silly shapes that wink and fly,\nLike a jester in a parade,\nBringing chuckles, unafraid.\n\nDancing with whimsy, up they go,\nFilling hearts with a radiant glow,\nTickled by the day's sweet tease,\nClouds chuckle in the playful breeze.\n\nWhen the sunset strikes the scene,\nEvery color wears a grin so keen,\nA carnival of hues involved,\nIn the sky, laughter resolved!

Glint of the Setting Sun

As the day waves a goofy goodbye,\nThe sun winks with a twinkling eye,\nGolden giggles stretch and yawn,\nNighttime's pranks are almost drawn.\n\nRaybands slip down, silly on the sly,\nFunny shapes dance, oh my oh my!\nCrickets chirp a little cheer,\nWhile the fireflies hover near.\n\nSunsets wear a jester's cap,\nThey flip and flop, a funny nap,\nColors in a playful spree,\nCrafting joy for you and me.\n\nWith a wink, the sun Is done,\nBut laughter lingers, oh so fun,\nAs night drapes its velvet sheet,\nIn this funny, cheerful retreat!

Firefly Embrace

In the garden, flickers bright,\nTiny beacons, pure delight,\nFlashes of giggles, twirling light,\nChasing shadows in the night.\n\nWith a wink and a gentle glow,\nFireflies dance, putting on a show,\nThey mock a star's funny bob,\nSwirling whispers as they throb.\n\nCatching dreams in glowing nets,\nEach laugh a spark we won't forget,\nBumbling around in silly glee,\nAn enchanting firefly jubilee.\n\nAs dusk fades into night's embrace,\nFireflies laugh in a glowing race,\nUnder this whimsical night sky,\nWe join the fun, just you and I!

Radiant Ember

A squirrel in shades, it's quite a sight,
Dancing on branches, full of delight.
He twirls and he leaps, not a care in the world,
Pine cones are thrown, as laughter is hurled.

A cat with a hat, prances around,
Chasing his tail, and wobbles abound.
He trips on a leaf, what a clumsy lad,
Yet his little antics make everyone glad.

The sun beats down with a cheeky grin,
Daring everyone to come out and spin.
Jump ropes are twirling, the children all shout,
"Catch me if you can!" as laughter rings out.

At twilight's call, the frogs start their song,
Croaking in chorus, how can they go wrong?
With a wink at the moon, they leap and they twang,
In this happy hour, everyone sang!

Sunset Whispers

A parrot in shades, not quite what you'd think,
Tells jokes to a crab who is sipping his drink.
They chuckle and squawk, a comedic pair,
While beach balls bounce high in the sun-drenched air.

The sandman's got moves, he's grooving away,
With flip-flops on, he dances all day.
Towel-wrapped folks join in with a cheer,
Even Grandma is busting a move here!

As the sky melts down in a colorful spat,
A dog with a frisbee thinks he's quite fat.
He leaps for the throw, but then makes a blunder,
And tumbles right back in a soft cloud of thunder.

The sunsets are whispers of laughter and fun,
As seagulls compete to steal hotdog buns.
With giggles and gasps, we savor the night,
'Til the stars pop out, and guide us with light.

Fiery Horizon

There's a clown in the park with paint so bright,
Riding a unicycle, what a silly sight!
He juggles some oranges, they bounce and they fly,
One hits a dog, who just gives it a try.

The wind has a tickle that makes everyone laugh,
Kites dance and flutter, what a playful staff.
A group of kids giggles as they tug at a line,
They send their kites soaring, a colorful sign.

At dinner time's call, the grill starts to smoke,
A chef with a mustache, he's part of the joke.
He flips hotdogs high, oh what a sight,
And catches a burger, much to our delight!

As twilight descends, the fun is not done,
With fireworks bursting, each pop like a pun.
Laughter and joy fill the sweet summer air,
In this lively tableau, we've nothing to spare!

Citrus Dreams

A funny old cat with a citrusy flair,
Wears a lemon hat, what a sight to bear!
Chasing sunbeams that slip through the trees,
He spins and he flops, if you please, if you please!

The kids in the yard play games with delight,
While water balloons soar, it's a splashy sight!
One lands on the dad, who lets out a yelp,
And the neighbor's dog joins in with a help!

As the sun dips low, the shadows grow long,
A fox strums a tune, and the frogs sing along.
With banjo and woes, they create such a scene,
In this slice of whimsy, what fun it has been!

Underneath twinkling stars, we share all our dreams,
With giggles and whispers, the night softly beams.
The world feels so bright, like a zestful delight,
In a citrusy glow that makes everything right!

Warm Lullabies of Night

When the sun takes a snooze, oh what a sight,
The skies play tricks, a true delight.
Crickets wear shades, chirping with glee,
The moon holds a party, just wait and see!

Stars wink like secrets, bright as can be,
Fireflies dancing, a light jubilee.
Nighttime's the time for giggles and fun,
When daisies tell jokes—oh, what a run!

A blanket of calm, so soft on the ground,
With laughter and whispers, oh, what a sound!
The cosmos giggles, it's cosmic flair,
While cats play the ukulele without a care!

So snooze on the grass, let dreams take their flight,
With warm lullabies chorus of night.
When dawn kisses orchards, all secrets will spill,
But for now, let the nighttime goodwill!

The Burning Edge

In the kitchen a pot, bubbling with cheer,
It spatters and sputters, oh dear, oh dear!
This soup's got a flair like no other can boast,
With vegetables prancing, oh what a toast!

The toaster pops up, throwing toast in the air,
Like it's auditioning for a flying affair!
Bacon's doing ballet, sizzling just right,
While eggs form a band, jamming through the night!

A commotion erupts, oh, who wants a bite?
Pancakes are flipping, such breakfast delight!
They whirl and they twirl, with syrupy friends,
In this kitchen of chaos, the fun never ends!

So grab a warm plate, let's feast like a king,
While the spatula dances and the kettle will sing.
Life's full of laughter, just not a dull edge,
In the culinary circus, we're all on the ledge!

Illumined Whispers

In the garden at dusk, fairy lights glow,
While daisies gossip, oh do they know?
Beetles are gossiping, sharing their tales,
While snails in top hats are raising their sails!

A glowworm's got style, a true little star,
Moonbeams are giggling, brightening the jar.
Tulips are swaying, doing a dance,
While wind plays a flute—oh, what a romance!

Crickets hold meetings in fractal-shaped leaves,
Strategizing laughs as the night softly weaves.
Each whisper a chuckle, each rustle a cheer,
In the enchanted garden, all's sunny and clear!

So prance with the petals and bop with the breeze,
Join in the laughter, if you wish, if you please!
These illumed whispers will carry you far,
In a world where each giggle's a shooting star!

Sunset Blossoms

At day's end, colors jump, what a scene!
The flowers start giggling, oh, aren't they keen?
Petals turning pink like a cheeky grin,
Photosynthesizing antics, let the fun begin!

A sunflower curtsies, sways to the beat,
While violets crack jokes, oh what a treat.
Daffodils chuckle, lifting their heads,
As the sun plays peekaboo from its cozy beds!

The breeze brings a tickle, a soft little nudge,
While marigolds blaze like they're set to judge.
In this garden gala, we're dancing in rows,
With colors exploding, let the laughter flow!

So let's spin and twirl in this sunset parade,
With blossoms and giggles, our worries will fade.
As day says goodbye, let joy take its flight,
In the hush of the twilight, all feels just right!

www.ingramcontent.com/pod-product-compliance
Lightning Source LLC
Chambersburg PA
CBHW070314120526
44590CB00017B/2673